ENNUI...

#FeelingsUnchained

Niru Rose

INDIA · SINGAPORE · MALAYSIA

ISBN
Paperback 979-8-88783-303-3
Hardcase 979-8-88783-568-6

I dedicate this book to my **Mom**, **Dad**, **Brother**,
all my **family**, & **friends**.

A special dedication to **Demetria Devonne Lovato**.

Contents

Preface

I have an endless love to comfort those in need & to inspire people to change for the better. Discovering the ability to do both these things in an elegant form called poetry.

I put forth my first poetry collection
"ENNUI... #FeelingsUnchained", a collection of quotes,
prose & poetry that has comforted some in need
and inspired some to change.

&

Always Remember.

"There's **no poem** *for* **everyone** *but,*
There is **someone** *for* **every poem...**"

Felt It (Or) Dealt It

1

Be The Real You

Your actions define you greater than your name,
body, mind & soul...

Not all times are alike, but you can change it if you like...

Nothing seemed pure
Made me very unsure
I began searching for a cure
To make everything pure

Only to realize, being impure
Doesn't need a cure
It's the secret sauce which makes sure
You are the way who you are...

It's not necessary to follow a path
You can always create your own path...

No amount of peace treaty
Will teach about inner beauty
That we all share in unity
But most prefer self-vanity

We're just souls
Trapped in bodies,
Of God's choice
Without a poise

You'll understand about equality
When you realize, everyone has a special quality
Hidden from the reality
In a beauty called humanity...

Everyone is different
That's what makes them special & unique
All have their own perfection of themselves
So don't force yours on them
Nor be forced by others
Find your own perfect self
"Be The Real You"...

I just wanna
Be free of this lacuna
I just wanna
Get rid of this stigma

I just wanna
Break free of the rules
Cuz, I just wanna
BE ME...

Boys can love pink
Girls can love blue
Remember, life is a rainbow
You should choose whatever color you love
Even if it's black & white...

2
Care

Busy is just a word for those you don't care enough...

I don't share
But tend to wear
Drops of tear
For those very dear
Coz I secretly care...

Sometimes we care
Of those very rare
For who even the things unfair
Turns into to something fair...

Each drop of tear,
Says that you care...

Don't say it with your lips,
show it with your heart...

When every feeling that's locked in
Gets hard for handling
I become maudlin
And need someone for cradling...

You may be judging
That I'm grudging
But I'm just sensing
Oddly cringing
A fear of losing
Coz I'm caring...

As much as you say
Don't worry about me
I keep questioning myself why
Can't I just stop caring
At least pretend to stop worrying...

3
Self-Harm

Don't blame yourself
Don't hurt yourself
It's not your fault
It's your environment's fault

Don't feel any shame
Your community is the one to blame
Please don't self-harm
I'm here to keep you warm

Even if you're unable to share
I'm here to care
At times life seems to be unfair
It's when you need to dare

There's no problem that's impossible to solve
All you have to do is, just give a chance to self-love
And you'll see as you change & evolve
All your problems will tend to dissolve...

4
Misfit

Water drops falling down
Like a needle rain
Skin piercing pain
Isn't enough to heal my deep down

Life of listlessness
A world of darkness
People call this the new normal
I just struggle to fit in so casual

With thoughts so dreary
Opening up is too scary
When nobody relates to your misery
You lose the ability to find the beauty...

Being a misfit
Is better than being a counterfeit
This world may not understand you
It doesn't mean, something's wrong with you
You are the key to the future
A whole perspective locked away
If you don't let It nurture
Everything special about you will wilt away...

5

Tears of Pain

Piercing through my vein
You continued to inflict pain
Trapped helpless in the rain
With you who seem so insane
As the rain muffles my cries
You sharpen your knives
To put me through a pain
That's worse than my bloody demise...

Time is stuck in an endless loop
Of every hurtful scoop
Causing Pain
Which's driving me insane
Bringing my worst fear
Of an endless tear
To come true...

6

Tears of Joy

When I bring a smile
On other's face
I'm immobile
With my heart rising its pace
& tears fighting to exile
From its birthplace...

When your dream
Is about to come true
Your eyes start to gleam
As the moment's finally here
All those years which were so mean
Doesn't matter now when all you want is so near
You would probably wanna scream
As your eyes burst out with tears...

7
BED Potato

Staying with me before I sleep
Staying with me when I wake
Singing me lullaby every night
Day and night by my side
Giving me warmth with a hug
All becomes so cozy and nice
I spent most of my time
Lying with you
My dear BED...

Like under a magic spell
I fell into a drowsy hell
With no strength to yell
Put in a hypnotic state to dwell
I wish to get well
For which time is what I need to sell
As my eyes compel
I'm gonna sleep, I tell
I'm gonna sleep, I tell...

8

Teacher

You learn today to teach someone tomorrow...

Tethering you to your path
Evaluating your worth
Accessible to your every ingress
Caring for your progress
Hides behind your success
Encouraging in your failure
Relinquishes when you find your own flavor...

9

Regret

I try my best to stay away from any expectation
As it's the source of every excruciation
But being something near perfection
It has a price called emotion
Don't you regret
That your life ain't perfect
You can't play cricket
Without losing some wicket...

I let you in
And confided in
Even when I knew,
We're bound to end

I fell for you
And it hurt me
I put trust in you
And you question me

Making me wonder
It would've been better,
To just love myself
Than to love you..

10

Mistake

Life isn't a clean slate
That has no mistake
It is something everyone will taste
In a process when you evaluate...

You're destined to ought
A life with some knot

If you haven't yet fought
You're yet to be taught
And yet to get caught

From which you may not
Easily escape of any sort...

If your heart ain't bubbling
Like your life's at stake
Even when you're crackling,
There's no worth for your mistake...

11
My Irene

It's the same old routine
Stuck in an endless quarantine
With everything unseen
Bound to be behind a social screen

Losing my sheen
For some prefixed pristine
Which is worse than a guillotine

I need to contravene
Though it might be a little mean
For my own Irene...

12

My Little Secret

Enclosed in a casket
My easter basket

Faith to my every belief
Always providing me relief

Source to my peace
Making everything at ease

Lighting up my face with a smile
Even when you are in exile

Removing me from my regret
My dear special little secret...

13
Self-Love

Searching for someone's appreciation
Eager for everyone's validation
Losing yourself for acclamation
Fooling yourself over affection

Lurking in your own fixation
Overwhelmed with anticipation
Vouch for your own elation
Exile any thought of desperation...

It was the time of walking dead
Lost in space and mind, to find
A tiny speck of solace in pain
To lie to yourself in faith
For hopes & dreams that
Aren't smoke & mirrors

Even hate is comforting than
Pushing through the pain of forgiving
Who could've ever imagined that
Even self love could be hurting...

14
Solitary

All of a sudden
I don't wanna be your burden
I feel so sorry
For the loss of your every merry
I just wanna be in solitary
Coz I don't want anyone to worry
It feels like I'm hurting
Even though you say it's nothing
When it comes to sadness
Solitude is my madness
I find it difficult to harness
The courage to share my darkness...

15
Maybe

Maybe it was my only chance
Maybe not,
Maybe it was for a change
Maybe not,
Maybe it would have been very strange
Maybe not,
Maybe it's my lack of courage
Maybe not,
This unknown possibility is taunting my rage
I'm gonna go on a rampage
It's causing too much damage
To lose my own image...

Maybe I'm still one of the fools
To believe in the existence of happy endings
Maybe I'm still naive
To believe in magic & fantasies

Maybe I wasn't hurt so bad
That I cannot feel anything else
Or maybe I still try to keep my hopes burning
Even though the world downpours on it...

16
The MOO Point

Too much is there to do
I don't know what I'm gonna do
Piling up all that's needed to go
All I do is stay at a point of MOO...

Until there's somebody to care
About what you're gonna share
Even if you have something coined
You'll still be in the MOO point...

17
Hopeless Heart

When I try to care for all
It always results in a bottomless fall
Though there's a solution so small
But it's not the right call

I'm unable to choose one over the other
Losing myself altogether
Coz it's hard to choose one (or) the other
When I want all to be together

This ain't no crumbly tart
Or a list to the weekly mart
To cut the unnecessary part
It's my hopeless heart...

I wish I could accept
It's just the fate
But it's just a concept
Of a giving up state
Though everyone would expect
To give in to the lightless night
I still couldn't accept
The night can swallow all of my light...

Losing a lot
Even though I fought
With everything I've got
Is something that's hard to get past

To get caught
And be taught
Is a God's plot
Which is a life's knot

But some part
Of my hopeless heart
Still hopes for the impossible 'not'
Even though I know, I've lost...

I know I'm hopeless
To still believe in fantasy
Even in this horrible reality
Hoping to find a speck of magic
Amidst this insanit...

18
Lonely

An unknown emptiness
Hovering in darkness
Spreading all kinds of madness
Reanimating each & every sadness

I'm unable to break
Even with my loudest shriek
When silence is at its peak
All my possibilities seem so bleak

An endless search for a company
Who can always accompany
Can't be bought with money
Giving a chance to experience true harmony

Nothing's ever lovely
Coz, when you're lonely
Even something sweet & heavenly
Will taste deadly...

Sitting in a corner so idle
With thoughts hard to handle
I wish time could become idle
To give me some peace to kindle

Sometimes we lose the saddle
And everything seems too hard to handle
But all you need is a loving cradle
To cross the baby paddle...

I tend to shroud
With nothing out loud
Though surrounded by a crowd
Lonely is what I've endowed...

I thought I was finally abode
But without anyone
It just showed
Me a pain of being all alone...

Oh, magical fairy
Why did you curse me this fury
That kills all my dearly
Leaving me empty and lonely...

19

Perfect Decoys

I'm lost in a world of noise
Struggling to find my own voice
Surrounded by nearly perfect decoys
I'm stuck here, unable to make a choice

Bit by bit being slowly erased of my entity
Left with no identity
I call upon every deity
Pleading to save me from this deadly calamity

Standing still in the bustling crowd
Like a corpse that's enshroud
Feeling like a land that's plowed
Broken, turned over & totally cowed

With an everlasting sense of incompleteness
Questioning the purpose of every existence
Isn't there an end for this madness
To be free of ever false kindness...

Just to please, though it makes us unease
We perform an act to ease
For which we pay a very high fees
Just to be part of a race
That never seems to seize
In which we live a life of multiple face...

20
Nuzzle

At times I'm baffled
With everything frazzled
All becomes a hassle
Though I live in a castle

Even the slightest rustle
Or a soft whistle
Makes me hustle
Putting me in an endless drizzle

But even the complicated puzzle
Flies like a tassel
When you snuggle
And hit me with a nuzzle...

21
Agony

I cannot stop this journey
Towards a peaceful destiny
Coz I deserve to be a little happy
After you made me a tragedy
Even though you say sorry
Or bring me a magical pony

My dear phony
Stop the tarry
I'm too weary
To continue your parody
Coz, you're causing an agony
Shattering my life's harmony...

I thought you'll be my future
But my future told you're my past...

Even the loudest shrill
Doesn't break the silence you left me in...

I'm just a symphony
With no harmony
Coz, it's my destiny
To face every agony...

I have fallen
Maybe not from heaven
But I've had my heart shaken
To have it silently stolen

My hopes to happen
We're simply broken
Leaving me forsaken
To be never taken

Now once again
I'm lost & going insane
Dreading to ride the pain train
All over once again...

22
Let Go

It's too much of a hassle
When you are too facile

You were my castle
But now just an abysmal
Of painful memories that rustle
Endlessly like a flying tassel

To be normal
As everything was casual
Feels rather unusual
And too hard to be perceptual

It's no point in holding on
When you need to fly again
It's time to let you go
So I could love again...

It's hard to let go
Even though you say let it go
I couldn't let you go
Nor the thought of letting go

It would have been easy
If I was a little bit sleazy
A lot less dreamy
And If you weren't cozy...

At the break of dawn
Let your problems be forgone
Hope there's no glimpse of one
When you've got past noon
Let there be joy & humming
As you bask your evening
Providing you the strength to fight
This lonely sleepless night
With horrors that's hard to let go
Entangled In memories
You don't wanna ever let go...

23

Weird Me!?

An Emotional Fool With A Hopeless Heart...

Why can't I talk without a reason??

Don't you start anything
And leave it incomplete with me
Coz, I'll haunt you until I know it all...

I love listening to other's problem,
Coz, it's my problem...

I love to help but hate to get help!!

Once I love, It'll be something I'll always love!!

24
Ego

Love was no longer a glue
To hold together which ain't true

If we had just let go
Of this stupid ego
And learn to fly low
When against the flow

There wouldn't have been a flaming rain
That burned us down with pain
All we built was lost in vain
As we, broke to be, one's gain

Is when 'we' were no more
And 'I' was born once more..

Petal by petal
In and Out
Day and night
Through the thorns
Together we bloomed
The rose of love

Little by little
As egos clashed
Everything else smashed
Smiles we lost
As silence casts
Without our care
Wilted our rose
Petal by petal...

25
Smile of love

Shattering the reality
With your smile of simplicity
Feeling of complexity
Overloading me with an intensity
My heart raises in density
Beyond its capacity

A strong sense of parity
In every calamity
Of a unique variety
Becoming my rarity
With a special quality
To make insanity
Shout out sanity
Adding a novelty
To my own identity...

I'll smile even on exile...

You, losing your smile
Is a source of my ail
To prevent it and prevail
I'll fight till my exile...

Your smile had me inspire
A love that thrive
Beyond time & couldn't expire
Even in my darkest deprive...

I'm effusively gushing
Uncontrollably blushing
Intensely crushing
On you, every time you smile...

Though we are worlds apart
You are still close in my heart
Through the stars at night
I see your smile so bright...

26
Power of Smile

A smile covers your cries
But your cries discover your smiles...

You don't see my cracks
Coz I paint it with my smile...

Try to bring a smile to other's face
Trust me it's totally addictive...

An innocent smile through your eyes
Makes me smitten
Overwhelming all my senses
Like a newborn kitten...

Whatever you may wear
Don't forget that, your smile
Is the best thing you can ever wear...

27
Buried

It made me worried
When I had everything buried

Even when I was harried
I still kept everything buried

Though I tried to be parried
At times so horrid
Since we're married
I still kept everything buried

Finally, now I'm carried
And about to be the one who's buried...

28
Emotional Hangover

You showed me the way to heaven
Right when it was about to hit seven

I fell right into hell
When you said it's over
And I was left with an emotional hangover...

The time that I wished it wouldn't end
Is the time when you were my seven heaven

The time, I now question when's the end?
Is the time when you became my burning hell....

29
Little Surprise

Every little surprise
You give me are my
Little bundles of joy

Bursting out love
Blurring out everything

My heart skips a beat
As you put a smile on my face
Even on my days in hell...

I fell for you
Not because of your beauty
Not because of your sweet words
It was the little details
Like getting the sugar in my coffee light
To getting the AC temperature to be just right
It showed me how much you love me...

30
Lemonade

Times of distress
Shredded into pieces

As you froze my burning sun
Without any gun
Giving me the energy to run
Turning everything into fun

Sweet (or) Salted
You always made everything sorted...

31
Life

Life is just the time,
We have left...

Tell me what to think
Tell me who to be
Tell me which to choose
Tell me whom to speak
Tell me why to do
Tell me how to live
Just like that, you take up
Your second life killing me...

What you are having now
Was once somebody's fantasy...

There's no good without bad
There's no smile without tears
There's no peace without struggle
There's no pleasure without pain...

There's always a choice
You only need the guts to take it...

It's okay to start things over and over but never give up on it..

From buzzing alarms
To figurative face palms
Life doesn't give something calm
There's always a storm
Waiting to hit
While you plan to sit...

It only takes, a second to change your life forever...

Flipping through the pages
It gets harder & heavier
To turn them over,
In a book called life...

People say death isn't a choice
But, we do choose to live
Every breathing second...

32
Words

You might've heard
The pen is mightier than the sword
It's not based on their sharpness
It's the words that are born out of a pen
Which has the immense power
To hurt the invincible
As well as
To heal the impossible
If it comes from the right person...

Words are powerful enough to
Create a change that never changes...

Sometimes, just words aren't enough to describe the experience...

When did words loose it's meaning?
When did they loose their value?
When did 'no' stopped meaning 'no' !?
When did 'love' stopped being 'love'!?

I don't rhyme,
I'm just a bunch of stupid words
Put together, for no reason
No purpose, just nonsense

When one single word triggers
A wide range of emotions
All other word's existence
Seems a little..a lot, pointless...

33
Refine

It's time to come out of the shade
And stop trying to evade
Cannot always hide
Every single time

Smiling in the outside
Shielding on the inside
It's time to let it fade
And to start on my parade...

It's beyond time
Yet I'm not in line
The thought of mine

Is shadowing my shine
To make it all fine
I need to refine...

34
Silent Cries

Believing someone's lies
You made your choice
Like a selfish novice
Shattering my hopes
Of everything nice
You brought me tears
And silent cries...

Things are sometimes harder to reveal
As sadness doesn't have much of an appeal
When you cannot explain what you feel
It just gets bottled up in a tight seal
And harder it gets to heal
As I'm unable to scream
Silent cries became my routine...

It's so hard to blink
And I need to think
Before it could brink
And I could completely sink
I badly need a drink
But all I could do now is just ink...

Is it something charming
Or else something harming
I'm simply calling
Coz it's really boring

Giving me a blow
Disrupting my flow
Making me slow
Removing everything that can glow
Like covered in snow
I'm, left with nothing to show

It's easy for just saying
When there's no point trying
This is just my silent crying
Hoping someone would be replying...

A huge sigh
So audible to deny
Masking my silent cry
To create a solid lie...

Even though the rain drenched me
On the outside, I feel dry when,
I'm sinking in my cries on the inside...

35
Perfectly Imperfect

I don't like to ask
So I make it my task
Never to lack
Or to look back

Removing the possibility of fear
Even with the one very dear
Though the pressure is so sheer
I don't crack (or) tear...

All my life I've done an inspection
To find every bit of perfection
But I've realized in every creation
There's a hidden beauty in every imperfection...

36

Sassy

Don't just follow to unfollow,
And remember I could do it too...

Life ain't full of daisy
It's always too hazy
When you're really lazy
To do something crazy

Being so sassy
Ain't mean you're classy
There's no point in being shady
Of you being crazy...

Don't like without reading,
Don't comment without meaning,
Don't share without feeling...

I don't really change due to others but,
I mess them up in my own special way...

You don't need authentication to enter my life,
But at least notify when you leave...

Think before you mess with me
Coz, the scares I cause
Ain't visible to the naked eye...

You don't deserve
The best version of me
If you can't accept
The other versions of me...

37
Rain

We fall to ensure your life
But you waste our life instead...

When life gives you rain
Add music to it &
Enjoy the shower...

Even though the rain drenched me on the outside
I feel dry when I'm sinking in my cries on the inside...

When you realize
Rainbows aren't just

Found outdoors,
In a blissful drizzle
With a warm sun's kiss

But they're also found
In a cold room
With a single white bulb

When seen through your
Cozy blanket & teary eyes...

I wish it rains everyday
To cover my tears
And make me smile
Washing away my sad little life...

38
Change

Change is the only thing that never changes
Throughout the ages
It has been consistent
Defying every existence...

Nothing remains the same
All changes in a little way
It's only a matter of fact
That we find it (or) not...

They say change is something that never changes
Even after so many changes you still are
My only constant...

39

Judgmental

To all those judging eyes
And a face that's faking smiles
You don't know my miles
Or seen my real smiles
Rumors may have lies
Overshadowing what really lies
In a world of likes
There's no place for being nice...

I do have my share of struggles
But I hide it safe in my twisted riddles
Coz I don't want you, to be part of my hurdles
So think before your judgmental mumbles...

Judge all you want,
There's a lot hidden from what you see...

40
Modern Love

In a life of pillows and walls
With silent cries and calls
Fantasies of happy endings
Brought me harsh realities

Love in fairytales
Is just false hope
The bliss of short tales
Is today's dope

In this hazy mess
Even light becomes darkness
Purity and innocence
Are just masks with incense...

It was all so perfect
And that was the sign,
I knew something was incorrect
Every time I called you mine

Yet I was too caught up
In the spur of the moment
And now all sums up
With the end of your whirlwind

I was simply thrown away
Once you had enough to play...

How can you say 'I love you"?
Even when we've never met
What kind of love is it?
Shallow & superficial

Even among all the words
I know love is very complex
But, you wouldn't even care
To know what it really means

As you throw it around blindly
Hoping to just get lucky...

41
Twilight

The dusk of light
The dawn of night
Blend a magical skylight
That's a feast to the eyesight

A little of sunlight
A little of moonlight
Making the perfect twilight

I wish I could freeze this time of delight
Beside you my mighty knight
Where everything is always alright...

Oh, your sparkly eyes
I don't just look at them
I fall into them,
Into a world of us
Where time seems irrelevant
As twilight shines endlessly...

One so warm
One so cool

Opposite in nature
Yet we met

For a brief moment
As we locked our gaze

To a time of twilight
Nothing else felt so right...

42

Fake Smiles

You don't have to tell it out loud
I see through your fake smiles
Even if you don't shout out loud
I could hear your silent cries...

As I put on a fake smile
To watch you walk away
Through the ashes under our feet
Burning the starry sky above our heads

My lips didn't say
You're the one
Cried my heart bleeding
Instead they put on a fake smile
To hide that feeling...

43
Wish

I wish I could offer you
A gown of a princess
I wish I could offer you
The crown of a queen
I wish I could offer you
Everything you desire
But for now
All I could offer is just me...

I wish I could offer you
A black-tie tuxedo
I wish I could offer you
The crown of a king
I wish I could offer you
Everything you desire
But for now
All I could offer is just me...

Wishes are special kisses
That break the limits
Of this society's hisses

At times a good luck charm
At times a sarcastical warm

It is a gentle kindle
For your hopes & desires

Making even the impossible
Seem so possible
And reachable...

44

Forlorn

Though our morning
Was filed with petty spat
It's you that I was missing
Like a forlorn cat
I keep on yearning
for your gentle pat...

Even though pillows & teddybears
Don't hug back
They never leave
Like people do...

45

Insomniac

I try my best to keep you open
But you shut me down with force
I drop my pen
As you tend to close

I lose control over me
And let you overpower me
In time I let go of the struggle
As you become an impossible hurdle...

46

Fine

Feelings of mine
Complicated, unstable & volatile.
Mood swings that even
I don't understand sometimes.

Doesn't have to be spelled out
To everyone, who asks
How you doin?

Most don't ever really care
About what you say
And to all those just say

I'm
Feelings that are so
Intense,
Never finding It's way to be
Expressed...

47
Fear

It has a huge history
Of being such a mystery
Gives you the chills
In spite of having the thrills

You taste it, when you have some
It's everyone's cumbersome
It's something you don't share
As it haunts you till you care
it crushes your desire
So that you get expire

There is a glitch
Even though you flinch
As long as you have a pinch
Of will, which is your hitch
To get pass this evil witch

It's just a
Feeling which
Everyone must
Acknowledge to
Rise high...

48

Hope

A ray of light through the dark room
Providing you with the assurance
Making you cross over the edge
To do the impossible
Holding you together in your struggles
Making you fight till your last breath
The weapon forged by your will & trust

Destroying your fears
Even in the darkest nights
Makes you the last warrior standing
Giving strength to win the war
With a brave heart

Gives you the endurance to hold on
Makes you shine brighter than any star
It is the only piece of light
That can keep you alright

It's just
Holding
Onto it
Persistently till the
End & Beyond...

49
Trust

Trusting is something which affects you
Mentally, Physically & spiritually
It's like a sheet of glass if broken,
Once shattered, It can't be fixed
Without any marks left behind.

Trust is the base of everything
Always trust truthfully
Give your trust to the deserved
And never let down those who trust you

It's just a
Test that
Reevaluates
Us
Several
Times...

50
Faith

A belief which gives you a relief
Entrust you with your trust
It needs no evidence
Only your confidence
With a little patience
Brings a smile to your face
When pain is what you only face

Lights up your hope
Even when everyone says nope
It survives with the slightest spark
And makes you create your own mark
It gives you the strength
To face your own death

All you need to do is
Forever
Abide it
Inquisitively &
Trust without
Hesitation...

51
Nuptial

It's my greatest pleasure
To have both of you, a priceless treasure
No need for countermeasure
When there is love that I'm unable to measure
For a future with nothing to worry
A future where you're not sorry
A future with only merry
Wish you both happy anniversary...

Like the imperfect pieces
Forming the perfect puzzle
Adore each other's special quirks
As it completes your life's puzzle...

52
Broken Promise

A hope of forever
Even if not together
To promise your happiness
Before mine

No need of broken promises
When you're hurting to keep 'em together
No need of false hope
When you're unable to figure it out yet

Let the hell of forever
Dissolve in the heaven of today
Filled with love, wrapped by love
And just love...

Broken promises,
Shattered hearts,
Looks like a waste of time
For those who doesn't have
Someone to call mine...

Remember promises can break
Which can make your world shake
Cuz, sometimes people do fake
For their own sake...

53
Over & Over

Why am I falling for you
Over & over
Why am I thinking about you
Over & over
Why do I wanna hold you
Closer & tighter, forever

Why do you possess the power
To hurt me deeper & harder
How do you make me feel
Weaker yet stronger
How do you make my heartbeat
Slower & faster
Why do you matter more than
Anything & everything
Over & over and over...

You keep on falling on me
And I end up catching you
Like a magnet,
we keep on attracting
Towards each other...

I don't know how you do it
Time after time
You make me fall

Over and over
In love with you

Without any glitter
Without any glister
You shine brighter
You sparkle better...

54
Snore

I'm sorry dear, I cannot ignore
How beautiful you snore
Cuz I hopelessly adore
It like a classic folklore

Even with your eyes closed & sedated
You held me captivated
As your hair danced with the wind
I realized that you were my godsend...

55
Unlove

I'm a lot terrified
By the thoughts fleeting my mind
What if they ever get petrified
Before it does, I wanna unwind

Oh, my dear beau
Even if I ever unlove you
Please, help me fallback in love
Once again with you...

I don't know why!?
I have a love obsession

Still, I hardly fall in love
But every time I fall in love
With a person or a thing
It has always lasted forever

I don't think I can ever unlove
If something like that ever exists...

56
Breaking Myself

I'm not usually the first pick
And too often fell so sick,
I wish all of this ends too quick
But time doesn't give a tick!!

Unable to talk the talk
Failing to walk the walk
Hating to ask help
I'm just breaking myself

I'm the start & the end of every problem I attain
There's nobody to blame or claim
The power of hurting myself!!

Bit by bit into countless pieces
To break & be broken
With a dreary desire, to rest & expire...

57
Dark Love

When did love, become so dark?
It was meant to be stark,
Does it have an evil twin?
Which feels like you've sinned
Was it the blinding haze?
That hid this monster's real face
So charming & bloody harming
Who break hearts, just to have a taste?

Making you suffer alone
In a world of pain
Unable to move, breathe or retreat
To what used to be a paradise
Enchanted in fairy tales
Like a beauty of lies,
A creator of countless cries
And soul crushing lives

Like any other drug it also gives a high
But why is it legal?
Even though its injurious to mind, body, & soul.
This dark love hides in a façade
Of something mesmerizing & divine
So, nobody realizes that we're forced
To live with this incurable disease...

58

Dark Circles

Behind your dark circles
I see your sleepless nights
I see your late-night struggles

Trying so hard not to weep
Binging on your favorite shows
To escape your reality foes

Some nights thinking about love
Some nights wondering how?
Even some nights feeling all alone
Unable to call anyone with your phone

And finally, you let it unveil
As you're so tired of trying to conceal...

You did not talk much
And I never asked or forced
Cuz I always learned
From your exhausted eyes...

59
Just Because

Just because
You've been around my entire life
Doesn't mean you can make all decisions for me

Just because
You want to be a part of my life
Doesn't make me want to be a part of yours

Just because
You love me
Don't force me to love you back

Just because
You showered me with love
Doesn't mean that you can drain me of it

Just because
You gave me happy smile &memories
You don't get the right to rob me of it

Just because
You helped to fix me
You don't get the right to break me...

60
Lost Spark

My life seems all to perfect
All balanced to be, just right
Yet I feel so wretched
Fighting a war, hidden from everyone's sight

Bits & pieces, with an unknown hollow
Needed a break from the sweet & mellow
To find my lost spark
I had to search, places too dark...

Thank you for the spark
That inspired to make my tiny mark

To set free of my cage,
To become a part of the change
To expand my range
Lighting up in exchange

To ignite the lost spark
Of millions in the dark...

61
Alter Ego

I wish it's possible
To experience everything
I wish it isn't impossible
To leave out nothing
To be able to have
An alter ego
Who is able to have
Everything that I don't

Choices without consequences
To be able to reset
To explore every interest
And exhaust all chances
Everyone needs an alter ego
To live life to the fullest in one go...

I have this hunger
To feed on sadness
A raging anger
That's pure darkness
My alter ego
That I couldn't let go...

62
Rebound Love

I may have not loved you enough
For you to stay long enough
I'm sorry for giving hopes
Without realizing it's end of my ropes
To heal through the pain is so hard
But to put someone
Through pain to heal is so mad...

I had a broken heart
And was hurting so hard,
You showered me with love
And I silently accepted it, somehow
You believed love was meant to bound
But I knew you were just a rebound

Yet I let you believe
Cuz I wasn't ready, to relive
Losing to love
So I faked falling in love

I know sorry doesn't make up
For me breaking up
But its my mistake to own up
And I hope you don't give up
On your idea of love
For the pain, I've caused you now...

63
Blind Hope

Just a blind hope
True or false
I never questioned it
Cuz, I felt it

Making me whole
Completing my soul
Balancing every imbalance
Making sense of every nonsense...

♡♡♡

When you truly love someone
You give birth to a blind hope
That fights against everyone
For your loved one

It drives you
To focus on their best
Even at their worst
You'd say I love you

It could be the super glue
That binds the relationship together
It could also hide the clue
For your heartbreak in the future
Only a few can blindly hope
Even after they reach the end of the rope...

64
Cosmic

When you realize the coincidences
In your thoughtless actions
And rediscover the little things

That were part of a cosmic plan
You'd just end up
Bursting into laughter...

You're like the stars
Bright, sparkly & present everywhere
Expressing yourself all times

But I'm like the moon
Hiding & revealing myself bit by bit
Sometimes lost to the shadows...

65

HRV

You became a part of me
Before I even knew your name
A long relationship that shines
In spite being, on & off a million times

Sharing a bond of incredible depth
You became a part, of my every breath
Guarding me against your kind
Infecting my body & mind

We were known to be one
As you don't leave me all alone
You make me breathe hardly
My dear lovely HRV...

66

Moon

Stars maybe bright
But moon has the might
To put on a smile so bright
Even though it's the one with no light...

Even my worst days
Become better
By your smile from above...

We don't appreciate the value
Of everything that's close by
Maybe that's why
All the clouds pass by
While I stand mesmerized by you...

67

Closer = Harder

I don't get closer to you
Cuz every little step
I give you, more power
To disrupt my life

You may never realize
The endless struggle
I go through, regretting
The choice of getting closer

Yet I can never go away from you
Cuz it's even harder
Than opening up to you...

68

Dead Words

Oh dear,
You said 'I Love You'
Yet it felt so cold and empty
You said 'I Need You'
Yet it felt so ordinary

You used all these wonderful words
Yet they don't feel as they should
And I know you mean well & good
But they feel, like a bunch of dead words

Without any soul
Without any emotion
No love or compassion
Something missing from making them whole...

If you can breakup
Over a single sentence
Makes me wonder
If you ever were in love...

69
Perfect Partner

Without any words
You read my thoughts
Even in your absence
I linger your presence

You make me smile
Even with your eyes closed
You walked the aisle
Even when the world opposed

Even in sadness
You never stopped to care
And brought happiness
For me to share

An irresistible charmer
A human Medal of Honor
My beautiful love monster
You are the perfect partner...

70
Crush

A beauty like the moon
That doesn't fade soon,
With your lovely tune
You made me swoon

Followed you like a shadow
Imagined our date on a meadow,
I'm still someone you don't know
Hoping to be your beau

I nervously blush
As my heart turns into mush,
As you said hush
Oh no!, I got a crush...

My dear secret crush
To you I may never confess
Cuz in your presence
I go into a state of eternal hush

You're the one who makes me blush
Daydreams of you gives me endless smiles
You make my heart turn into a mush
You're the only reason to my countless
Heart skips & heartthrobs...

I don't know what it is
But it feels, a little good
I don't know what it is
Just, a bit anew

Words breaking my hush
Thoughts making me blush
Is this a crush?
Or just a love rush..?

I understand now
Why do words rhyme

As I blush
Before my crush
Silently I wish
For a surprise kiss
And I hopelessly miss
The moment you vanish...

71
Final Goodbye

Heavy breaths
Thoughts of distress
Unable to voice
This dreadful choice

You showed me love
And you taught me how
Yet I steal your happiness somehow
So it's time to stop it now

I'm sorry to defy
No longer can I deny
Oh the apple of my eye
This is my final goodbye...

It takes courage
To lose someone you love
But to save someone you love
Courage & the will to sacrifice is necessary

Not everyone Is capable of
Bidding away a final goodbye
To the one's they truly love
As they share a forever part
In our memories...

72
Anxiety

Who knew a single
Yes / No question
Can be this nerve wracking...

SILENCE
Does not give you peace, but
SILENCE
From the person you love
KILLS IT...

Maybe words don't posses the power,
The people using them does...

YOU
Possess the power
To bring JOY
To cause FEAR
To give COMFORT
To catalyze ANGER
And somehow LOVE...

73

Messy Me

I'm sorry dear
I'm totally childish
Unreasonably foolish
And you have to bear

The temper tantrums
That's so random,
I also uncontrollably tear
With the silliest of fear

Wondering if I could ever confess,
To someone, how much of a hot mess
I am...

Questioning the very existence
Searching for my quintessence
Getting lost in this world's madness
Surviving in drops of kindness

With layers to undress
& fears to confess
Need a soul to process
The hidden beauty of my mess...

74
Darkness

Your over brightness
Is hurting & blinding
I just need some darkness
Cuz, it's so comforting...

There's always a light
At the end of a tunnel they say
There's aways a special place
In your heart you say
You shower me with love
Yet I'm so terrified of it
You wanna be a light in my life
And I know what you feel is so pure
But I don't know why I choose darkness
Over light every single time
I'm just comfortable when I'm sad
But never peaceful when I'm happy

To have happiness
Means to be able to loose happiness
And its painful than sadness

And a lifelong darkness
Maybe light shines brighter
In the darkness
But darkness just exists quieter
Without light, forever eternally...

75
Chemical Love

Don't ever come into my life
In the name of love
It's just a distinguished knife
Aeons long intricate bluff

Designed to deceive
Spelled to seal
You ache to receive
This curse, to feel

Love is just
A bunch of feel good chemicals
Giving a temporary high

It's withdrawal is deadly
And its overdose messes you up
For an eternity...

76
Scarred

You're making me regret
For letting you in,
I wish I could forget
But it feels like a sin

You used to be my home,
To bring peace, at ease
It's now a place I'd never come
Cuz, every time you're breaking off a piece

I'd never thought that I'd feel
Hate towards you, even if I had to pretend
But when I felt it for that second
I was scarred, & it'll never heal

Only if I could control my tears
Shut close my ears
Distance you like a stranger,
Only then I'll survive this danger...

77

You

Once again you came into my life
In one glance, I stood frozen
Mesmerized & paralyzed
By your breathtaking beauty

Just by existing
You make my life so exciting
Smiles that make me hurt
Tears that make me melt

You give me the reason
To be a better person
To breathe in hate
And to breathe out love...

You're the source of every temptation
You're the reason I seek redemption
My one & only addiction
A special limited edition
And my lifetime subscription...

You held me captive
In my own mind
You had me captivated
Making everything else go blind

And I don't know why
I'm wishing you to be
My everyday morning alarm
And my night's lullaby...

You are the light
To my endless night
You are my knight
In a shining armor, that's too bright

You held me tight
You held me light
When nothing is right
You still make me aright

You share my plight
Silently and quiet
Even when we fight

You never, have ever, let me out of your sight
You never, have ever, let me out of your sight,
Let me out of your sight...

78
Philophobic Me

I will test your patience
Question your notions
Wreck havoc on your emotions
And exhaust you in the process

To simply sum it up
I'm so hard to love
And I suggest you
To give it up...

Love was inevitable
Said the philophobic me...

Your flaws break my laws
Yet I tend to whitewash
I don't know its cause
You make my time pause

There were a million reasons not to
Yet I was searching for just a reason
To hold on to...

79
Hitomebore

Like a butterfly flapping its wings
To create a storm somewhere
You gently blink your eyes
To create a storm in me somewhere...

Oh, I didn't know
I wasn't whole
Until I saw you
You touched my soul
Made me feel whole
And became 'the one'
From unknown

You're the only thought
Who won my heart
My dear missing part
See through my soul
It's where you rule
My angel of love...

80
Dear Highness

I choose to spend time with you
But I don't know, if I love you

I do love what we could do together
But I don't know, if I could choose you altogether

You shed new light to my life
You taught me the beauty of a lie

You showed me the brightness
You showed e the darkness
You showed me the happiness
Hidden in every sadness
You showed me the madness
You showed me the kindness
Why'd you choose me, my dear highness?

I'm now speaking in silence
Seeing you in every substance

Thinking with you in conscience
Wondering if you're the reason to my existence...

81

Saying NO

It's a struggle to say no
The very first time
But when you are
Forced over and over
It's do easier to give in
Rather than filling yourself
With self doubt & remorse...

♡♡♡

In hopes of helping
You're just hurting
You are abundantly caring

That's why you're overpowering
Even when I say no you're ignoring
I don't have the energy to start arguing

I know you're ready for hearing
But I'm not ready for speaking
Cuz, I need time for healing...

♡♡♡

When you keep giving up
Your life to others
And their problems

Wondering how to stop
Without feeling guilty
Of not being there for someone

Maybe it's okay to say
A no once in a while

If only that was so easy...

82
Lost

Sometimes I just get lost
Into your eyes
Losing track of time
As my heart tingles
I forget my surroundings
Into a world of magic
That's wrapped in love
Where logic doesn't apply...

I'm lost like a needle, in a haystack
And you're the magnet that guides me home...

Loosing my sunshine
Led to this moonshine...

83
Sorry

Sorry for hurting you
I didn't know what to do
When you kept on hurting me
While I'm trying to explain how you're hurting me
I know sorry is not gonna make things right
But what better ways are there to make things right..?

I know you are sorry
I know you worry
But things so dreary
Needs time my dearie

I'm trying my best
To free my heavy chest
But I couldn't put it to rest
Like a cursed treasure chest...

Thanks that's not felt
Sorry that's not meant
Are just better, when not said...

Please don't say sorry
When you don't know why
It's not the word that changes things for better
It's the hope of you not hurting me
Once again, that does the healing...

Don't let go
Is what I said
But I let go
Before we're dead

I could say i'm sorry
But it ain't gonna change your worry
Coz to loose everything dearly
Is really pretty scary

I broke your trust
And everything we've invest
Into this relationship
That I sunk with you in it...

84

No more

No more love to give
No more time to share
No more energy to waste
No more tears left to shed

I'm done being selfless
It's time to become careless
A little bit too selfish
So that I don't perish

Hurt or broken
I ain't gonna worry
Sorry not sorry

I don't do that anymore
Cuz, I can take no more,
NO MORE!!, NO MORE!!!

85
Photograph

Photographs are not the memories
They're just bookmarks to it
So cherish every special moments
With a bookmark
Cuz life is all about the journey
Not the destination...

Photographs may cease to exist
Resemblance may dies to persist
I'll never need those to remember
You, my invaluable treasure
A blessing for which I'll thank forever...

86
What's Life?

Is it to chase a dream
Is it to get settled down
Is it checking out a bucket list
Or is it falling in love
What is life?
I wonder
What is it all about?

A little voice in me said
It is a time frame of your presence
In this world either
Physically, Mentally, Spiritually
Through words, songs, or memories
And in every breath you take in...

87
Mad Love

Mystery that's unexplainable
Magic that's inexplicable
Moments that are unforgettable
Miracles become easily possible

When you have someone
To love you back
As madly as you do
As hopeless as you do...

All that U ever wished for
Is to have, all your wishes fulfilled
No matter how intricate
No matter how explicit
No matter how illicit
It seals my eternal fate...

88
Time Capsule

Stuck in a time capsule
Hoping the days of the past
Would make sense in the future

The future thought me
Stop wondering
About your past and future
Focus on your present
As it's the only time you get to experience...

Kisses of kindness
Amusing every sadness
Versatile than vastness
Idealistic goodness
Toxic cuteness
And my adorable madness

Moments with you
Opens up something new
Memories we share
Outshines time too

Shadow of me was jealous
Hearing about the bond we share
Every moment with you seem so precious
Restlessly when you care
Unique you are my dear...

89
The Walk

On a not so perfect evening
The sun was quick to do it's hiding
Painting the sky black
While the cold winds blew through the shack

It might've been
What I would've seen
But, your very presence
Transformed its every existence

I was pretending to walk while having a fall
The walk slowly turned into a stroll
Breaking down each other's last wall
Creating a moment, that had it all

The clouds froze their droplets
To shower us with snowflakes
The half moon is waning away
To put on its shining smile our way

Walking hand in hand
As our fingers intertwined
Our heartbeats synchronized
And our should were finally pacified

Even the word love
Doesn't seem enough somehow
To describe this moment now

Sharing silent whispers
Denying to disperse
Getting a lot closer
Feeling a lot safer

With our eyes
Carrying each other's reflection
Hoping this path would never cease
To prolong this very sensation

Even our watches
Forgot to tick
Killing all our chances
Of ending this evening quick...

90
Cryptic

I'm encrypted
Are you the key to
My decryption..?

I'm a tangled mess
Unable to confess
Yet somehow you harness
The love to make us...

You may have entered
My life for a reason

You may have left
My life for a reason

How could I charge you a treason
Just because I don't get to
Know the reason...

91
Fragile Heart

My dear fragile heart
I know you get hurt a lot
Even for words so soft
You're making my life so damn hard...

I have a glass heart,
It's beautiful when whole,
Not shattered...

I thought you knew me better than this
Maybe it's my fault
To believe in my thought
So I wouldn't have bought any of this

Now I'm hurt
Cuz I was foolish enough
To believe you wouldn't hurt
Finally I realized it was just a bluff...

92
Galaxies Apart

Near or far
Distance doesn't separate us
When our thought are
Always connecting us

You are my daydream
Making my eyes gleam
Soft & sweet as a whipped cream
You gently make my heart scream

Oh, my dear obsession
You have stolen all my attention
With all my affection
Please take me under your possession...

Though I'm your unknown
You strangely affect me
More than my known...

Though we are worlds apart
You are still close in my heart
Through the stars at night
I see your smile so bright...

I've started to crave
For the taste of love,
Even beyond the grave
I couldn't find the one who could save

Someone who could freeze my thoughts
Someone for who I'm ready to take the fall
Someone who could make me to stare
Someone who could change it all

I don't care what's your name
I don't care what's your shape
Whatever may be your state
All I care is, what you feel, up to date

I'm sorry I couldn't see you
I'm sorry I couldn't hear you
I'm sorry I couldn't touch you
All I could do, is feel you
I don't know who are you
I don't know what are you
I don't even know where are you
All I know is, you are a part of me de I am a part of you...

93
Warm & Fuzzy

Tone winds whisper your name
Even the silence knows your fame
My thoughts are filled with your face
As my heart beats, in love's pace

Just your gaze
Traps me in daze
You steal away my pain
Like a sudden rain

I never knew heart could melt
Until you showed me how it felt,
One of life's greatest blessing
The warm fuzzy feeling...

94
Is Love!!

To feel
hell on heaven &
A heaven on hell
Is Love!!.

Getting yourself hurt
Cuz you don't want
Your special person to feel hurt
Is Love!!.

When seconds,
Feels like years
And years, feels
Like seconds
Is Love!!.

Me giving you
The power to hurt me
In the hopes of you
Never using it on me
Is Love!!.

95
Ennui

A sense of ennui,
Throughout my body, mind & soul.
I get lost into nothingness as
Dusk & dawn pass by
Questioning my existence
In the vast space of universe
What am I?, who am I?, why am I?

When there's nothing excites you
Nothing makes your heart skip a beat
Everything loses its lack & luster
The world is monotonous & boring
And all you do is search

Behind every search of passion
There's a sense of ennui...

Less Rhymey & More Wordy

96

Perfection: A Flawed Theory...

Most of my life I've searched for **'ultimate perfection'**. Questioning anything and everything to reach perfection. Being superficial even to the tiniest flaw. To a point where even the invisible flaws drive me crazy to replace them. But perfection to one person doesn't mean perfection to all. Everyone has a different level of perfection as **'no cup of tea is perfect for all'**.

So, there is nobody capable of knowing & satisfying my standards of perfection at everything except myself. This puts me in a constant state of worry, as perfection slowly became a necessity that I could now live without. Controlling me, rather than me controlling it.

Little by little I felt like I'm losing what's important & focusing on things that weren't important. Even though things being perfect gives me relief and is capable of putting a smile on my face, but it never lasted long enough before the next imperfection catches my sight. The process robbed me of my happiness nor gave any real connection to people around me. You cannot dispose people just because they don't meet your standards. People are not a mass-produced product but a uniquely designed, specifically trained signature edition.

'Each one is one of a kind'.

We all must realize humans are made imperfect. Imperfection is what makes us different from anything that seeks perfection. We aren't machines that have no feelings coz these feelings are what that makes the difference, and they are the reason to say we are human. The search for perfection at everything is a quest to lose humanity for an inhuman life, without any human connections that are real and mean something, nothing gives meaning to life.

As perfection varies to everyone, it isn't a universal standardized unit it's just a variable that varies on the base of an imperfection called **'feelings'**.

"It is
Imperfectly Perfect & Perfectly Imperfect
At the same time."

97

Modern Communication: Usually Less Meant of What's Said...

Through communication has evolved a lot from sign language to virtual communication. Verbal communication has always been a powerful way as well as the easiest way too. In today's world, not everyone is effective at speaking. Many prefer other methods than this, but the truth is nothing can replace a person's face to face verbal conversation (nor) mimic, its exact effect Sadly some doesn't have the gift of experiencing it at all. Even though it's the most used method of communication most of them really don't know the power it holds.

They seem to use the words without any care & never really mean what they say most of the time. Everybody has done it at some point in their life. It may be the words you've told to others (or) what you've said to yourself. Many of the people also know that they don't mean it, but it not always has a positive effect sometimes it even wrecks someone completely. As most wouldn't care about it as they tend to just forget it so easily because it was never from their heart. Eventually, it develops as a habit& it starts to get difficult with the people you care about as anger is the most common situation this occurs.

The problem here is that the people who care about you take your words to T and they don't just hear it through an ear & pass it out through another but take it to the heart even though you don't mean them sometimes. When you tend to say things that you don't mean, out of anger it hurts them bad even if you don't mean it, it hurts very bad especially when it comes from someone they love. It's always better to never say what you don't mean. As they say, words hurt you more than anything else in the world.

The most misused word today is **"Love"**. As due to its too much usage the word nearly lost its meaning. People have even started using it to just manipulate people, leading them on, building hope just to break which only leads people to question love, not the people. Just understand **'love'** isn't something you fall out of **'fast'** if you are truly in love with someone. This might raise a question is falling in love fast possible? It is but I think everybody must know how to test it. That's the only way you're gonna be sure. If you're continuously putting the needs of your loved one before yours and if the person you love does continuously prioritize your needs before theirs it means you are more important than themselves. That is the base of love. So, I'd say it's better to never say what you don't mean coz words have the power to either make (or) break you.

"Remember it is only as powerful as you want it to be"

So always try to take the everything (or) at least negative things lightly even though it's very hard to.

98

Stereotypes: A Pre Judgmental Identity

Stereotypes of any kind just robs the person of a fair chance to express themselves completely. This is a pre judgmental identity that is assumed of a person belonging to a social group. This stamp which has been passed down generations as a branding to someone that has been yet to be born. It often instills a fear of being misjudged no matter what causes people to be finicking over their every action giving them a social anxiety among any new groups of people.

"Stereotypes are an unfair trademark
That needs to be forgotten"

To put on a label on someone or a group of misfits is an easy thing to do. But it not just gives them an identity they never asked for but also brands them for generations and this process off labelling has never seen has a huge issue. The people who label others never really experience the repercussions of their thoughtless act.

Tattoos may fade, scars of fire may heal but a branding of words is undying, carried on even after your death. These stereotypes that have been passed on for centuries have to be eradicated. We should believe in seeing the person for who they are and not judge them based on any of their appearance, place of origin or a group of society.

Each person has travelled their own journey, not everyone can know it but to judge them based on any factors above would be like robbing them their freedom to paint a picture about themselves. Instead, we end up creating a common picture which could've been a masterpiece only if the opportunity wasn't robbed by us.

"Only a blank canvas can discover the truest beauty with ease."

Try to keep an open mind and a open heart towards everyone. As this allows you to get to know the real self of someone.

99

Equality: Beyond Gender, Race, Caste, & Creed.

Equality may be the buzzword of the 21st century. But that doesn't mean everyone understands it completely. It's not just a cry for help by the people who have been suppressed for years. It is a struggle for freedom that demands the basic needs of human to be given to all equally and not to be treated any less than you or me.

"Like snowflakes all are uniquely made
Beautiful in their own way
Yet they break like all."

Equality is a basic privilege that everyone irrespective of their gender, race, caste, & creed should obtain. Refusing it is as good as stealing their life from them. If we are not able to see each other as one and same we are on a path to losing humanity, the very thing which makes us enlightened than other beings on this planet.

True equality is only attained when people are seen through all the physical mirages and given a judge mental free chance to just express themselves freely. Everyone in this world deserves a fair shot at the world. It's just cruel to deny people of what's theirs just because their real self is so complex for you to understand or it's something you haven't seen before or even imagined to experience ever.

This world is hurting and needs a lot of unconditional love to heal itself. It's our duty as people to revive this world from the pain it has been put through by us. Contrary to the fact that healing this planet lies in planting more trees and preventing plastics and carbon emission. The real healing starts only when people get to see others as their equals and give them respect and love irrespective of their physical, mental and emotional state.

"Humanity without humans can exist
Humans without humanity should not..."

Don't let this & future generations lose the best part of being human. Their humanity!!.

My Poetic Diary

100

An Ode to Aredvi Sura Anahita

JAN 22

The sight of you 'LITERALLY'
Slowed down the time around me
Flashing my busy mind
To go blank
With your very presence
You took away my breath in an instance
Too close to feel
Yet sooo far in real
Totally,
It wasn't your fault
But,
Somehow you made me get lost...

JAN 23

You had me all smitten
You had my heart bitten
Oh my dear cute kitten
I cannot still pretend

Yesterday your presence
Took my breath away in an instance
Today your absence
Made me question my very existence

Searching for you
In the vast darkness
Missing you
Is driving me into a madness...

JAN 24

Where are you?
What are you?
I don't know
Why am I missing you!?

Everything feels so different
After that special incident
Which changed me altogether
FOREVER

You made an impression
Without any expression
You became an exception
To my every perception...

JAN 25

It has been 3 days
Since I've seen your face
Which lights up any place
Like the stars in outer space

Every single second
I yearn for you harder
I hope this wouldn't be the end
Of you & me together

Who ever knew that, you
Would have such an impact on me
Maybe it was meant to be you
(Or) it's just the crazy me...

JAN 26

Are you doing the 3 day rule?
(Or) am I an hopeless fool
It might be too soon
But, I don't wanna miss you my boon

I may sound a bit cheesy
But, the past days weren't so easy
As you made my view so hazy
That I see you everywhere, Hope I'm not just crazy

Where are you?
How are you?
Though I'm far from you
All I think about is only you...

JAN 27

With you in mind
I'm still on a search to find
That smile you shined
Which made me nearly blind

I'm roaming restless
Anxiously so sleepless
Coz I couldn't be so careless
To lose you my dear sweetness

3rd may not be the charm
5th may not be the charm
Inspire all the harm
You'll still be my lucky charm...

JAN 28

Even if I get swallowed by darkness
Driven crazy by madness
Filled with complete sadness
Your smile, will be my hope of light to harness

Giving me the strength to move forward
Even at times when I'm cornered,
Broken (or) even shattered
Your thought is my only comfort

Will I ever find you?
Will I ever see you?
I don't know anything about you
But, for now I very badly miss you...

JAN 29

A week has past by
Yet, you aren't anywhere nearby
All I hope is
This wouldn't be a goodbye

Day after day
I was searching for you
Week after week
I'll still search for you

No matter how long
No matter how far
I don't think I can stop
Until I meet you again...

JAN 30

To be honest, I'm losing hope
Of seeing you again
I don't know if I could cope
With all of this tormenting pain

Though my efforts end up in vain
I'm trying, not to go insane
Like the life giving rain
You keep me sane

There's no gain
Without any pain
But, I couldn't explain
Love's intricate game...

JAN 31

What can I say
Other than the fact
That you changed my life
FOREVER

One little incident
A happy accident
Broke my every resistance
Became my greatest influence

Though time may pass slowly
And I miss you so badly
I couldn't stop to fancy
YOU...

FEB 1

If giving up was an option
Nobody would've gotten anything
As you ain't something common
I'm not gonna stop even at ends of everything

My short and sweet haiku
Without you my life doesn't continue
If I ever see you
I don't think I can ever leave you

You're a light in darkness
My only happiness
You're a bundle of cuteness
My diabetic sweetness...

FEB 2

Near (or) far
Distance doesn't separate us
When our thoughts are
Always connecting us

You are a daydream
Making my eyes gleam
Soft & sweet as a whipped cream
You gently make my heart scream

Oh my dear obsession
You have stolen all my attention
With all my affection
Please take me under your possession...

FEB 3

The world seems a lot darker
Without you my dear
Instilled by a fear
Of losing you forever

A sudden sadness
An unknown madness
Infecting my thoughts
Infesting all my parts

Into a torment
Every single moment...

FEB 4

The time seems to take away the oxygen
To my candle of hope,
Burning lighter & dimmer
While everything is getting darker & colder

All of a sudden
My faith seems like a joke
Since this being a blind pursuit
Maybe the painful truth

Even if I'm against the odds
Even if it breaks my heart
The search doesn't stop
Until I find it all...

FEB 5

I cannot quit
Nor simply sit
I just couldn't forfeit
Nor find any exit

Oh fading hope
Don't get lost in smoke
You're the only rope
Helping me to say nope

To all the crazy little voices
Saying me to leave back without any trace...

FEB 6

It's been more than a fortnight
Yet I haven't given up the fight
Coz until tonight
You're to me the most beautiful sight

Reliving that special moment
Again & again & again
Hoping it to happen, in the present
So I don't miss you again

With love in the air
I do feel more romantic to be fair
You're the only one with you I could share
My life, and probably the most I care...

FEB 7

It’s the Rose Day
Yet I am searching for a way
To find you, to see you
To show that how much
I miss you

Wishing for a valentine’s magic
I gather roses of all kinds
To prevent any tragic
After all, you’re my rarest finds...

FEB 8

Oh my Oh my Oh my!!!
Finally, I found you
That shining smile
Could send me on an exile

Here I am proposing
To share a love that's ever growing
To share everything
Even If Its nothing...

FEB 9

I wish it was my fate
To have you as my date
Your memories have an after taste
Like a saccharine chocolate

Mesmerizing me in to a daze
Oh my dear honey glaze
I miss your face
And Its not a fleeting phase...

FEB 10

My adorable blue bear
It's you that I only care
Given the choice to be anywhere
I'd choose to be beside you somewhere

To be present In every Instance
As you are my purpose of existence
Awaiting you're acceptance
I'm using all of my persistence...

FEB 11

Even the stars don't live forever
But I wish my promise Is forever
To you, to my love
To be a part of you somehow

To be there for you always
In the sunny daze
(or) the midnight haze
You'll be In my thoughts always!..

FEB 12

Sorry dear if I've forced
It's because I was so confused
I now understand your hesitance
Sorry for forcing through your resistance

Its time to stop chasing
To get my heart back to its normal pacing

But I heard my racing heart
When you put your skipping heart
Behind mine & said it's all fine...

FEB 13

I'm filled with anticipation
Exhausting every perception
A day of restless & fluttering sensation
Might've been a secret temptation

With sparks too hard to miss
We had our first kiss
A moment of bliss
To be frozen in time, I wish!..

FEB 14

My lovely valentine
My eternal sunshine
My whimsical moonshine
My one & only lifeline

Like the sea & its seashores
Like the cloud & its rain showers
Like the meadow & its flowers
Like the fire & its embers

I'm yours as you're are mine &
You're mine as I'm yours...

Until Next Time...

NIRU ROSE

www.ingramcontent.com/pod-product-compliance
Lightning Source LLC
LaVergne TN
LVHW050546160826
845677LV00011B/2199

9798887833033